MY BOD

MY BODY HA

MOUTH

AMY CULLIFORD

A Crabtree Roots Plus Book

CRABTREE
Publishing Company
www.crabtreebooks.com

School-to-Home Support for Caregivers and Teachers

This book helps children grow by letting them practice reading. Here are a few guiding questions to help the reader with building his or her comprehension skills. Possible answers appear here in red.

Before Reading:

• What do I think this book is about?
  • *I think this book is about the things I use my mouth for..*
  • *I think this book is about the sounds that come out of my mouth.*

• What do I want to learn about this topic?
  • *I want to learn about the different parts of my mouth.*
  • *I want to learn about ways to take care of my teeth.*

During Reading:

• I wonder why...
  • *I wonder why I have so many teeth in my mouth.*
  • *I wonder why I have a tongue.*

• What have I learned so far?
  • *I have learned that I can use my mouth to sing.*
  • *I have learned that a dentist is a person who looks at my teeth.*

After Reading:

• What details did I learn about this topic?
  • *I have learned that I should brush and floss my teeth every day.*
  • *I have learned that my tongue helps me taste food.*

• Read the book again and look for the vocabulary words.
  • *I see the word **dentist** on page 16 and the word **floss** on page 17. The other vocabulary words are found on page 23.*

You have a **mouth**.

It is part of your face.

You use your mouth
to talk.

Your mouth can show
what you are feeling.

You can smile when
you feel happy.

You can frown when
you feel upset.

I use my mouth to sing!

You have two **lips**.

I use my lips to
kiss my mom!

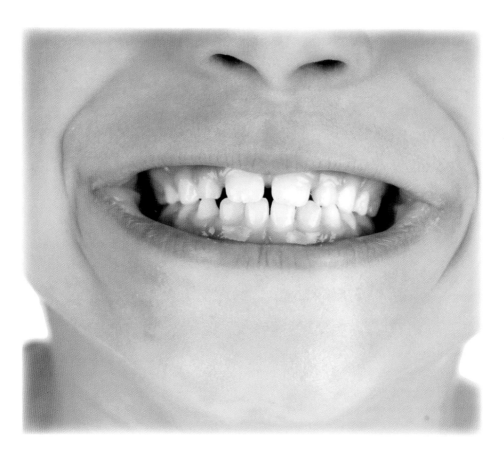

You have **teeth**
in your mouth.

Teeth help us eat
and chew food.

Open wide! A **dentist** looks at your teeth.

I brush and **floss** my
teeth every day!

Your **tongue** is in
your mouth.

Your tongue helps you taste things.

I use my tongue to make a silly face!

Word List
Sight Words

a	help	silly
and	helps	sing
are	I	smile
at	in	talk
brush	is	taste
can	it	things
chew	kiss	to
day	looks	two
eat	make	us
every	mom	use
face	my	what
feeling	of	wide
food	open	you
frown	part	your
have	show	

Words to Know

dentist

floss

lips

mouth

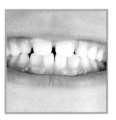
teeth

tongue

MY BODY
MY BODY HAS A
MOUTH

Written by: Amy Culliford

Designed by: Rhea Wallace

Series Development: James Earley

Proofreader: Janine Deschenes

Educational Consultant: Marie Lemke M.Ed.

Print and production coordinator:

Katherine Berti

Photographs:
Shutterstock: Rido: cover, p. 3; Veronica Louro: p. 4, 14; wavebreakmedia: p. 5; Krakenimages.com: p. 7; Nordic Studio: p. 8; Johm Roman Images: p. 9; paulaphoto: p. 11; Toey: p. 12; ffoto29: p. 13; Samuel Borges Photography: p. 15; Kinga: p. 16; Bon Nontawat: p. 17

Library and Archives Canada Cataloguing in Publication

Available at the Library and Archives Canada

Library of Congress Cataloging-in-Publication Data

Available at the Library of Congress

Crabtree Publishing Company

www.crabtreebooks.com   1-800-387-7650

Printed in the U.S.A./CG20210915/012022

Published in the United States
Crabtree Publishing
347 Fifth Avenue, Suite 1402-145
New York, NY, 10016

Published in Canada
Crabtree Publishing
616 Welland Ave.
St. Catharines, Ontario L2M 5V6